# This and That

# THIS AND THAT

A Tea-and-Biscuit Philosophy on
Life and the Law of Attraction

Rose Todd

Illustrations by Judith MacKay

www.paintingwithjudith.com

**BALBOA**
PRESS
A DIVISION OF HAY HOUSE

*Copyright © 2012 Rose Todd*

*All rights reserved. No part of this book may be used or reproduced by any means, graphic, electronic, or mechanical, including photocopying, recording, taping or by any information storage retrieval system without the written permission of the publisher except in the case of brief quotations embodied in critical articles and reviews.*

*ISBN: 978-1-4525-5307-8 (sc)*
*ISBN: 978-1-4525-5308-5 (e)*
*Library of Congress Control Number: 2012909583*
*Balboa Press books may be ordered through booksellers or by contacting:*

*Balboa Press*
*A Division of Hay House*
*1663 Liberty Drive*
*Bloomington, IN 47403*
*www.balboapress.com*
*1-(877) 407-4847*

*Because of the dynamic nature of the Internet, any web addresses or links contained in this book may have changed since publication and may no longer be valid. The views expressed in this work are solely those of the author and do not necessarily reflect the views of the publisher, and the publisher hereby disclaims any responsibility for them.*

*The author of this book does not dispense medical advice or prescribe the use of any technique as a form of treatment for physical, emotional, or medical problems without the advice of a physician, either directly or indirectly. The intent of the author is only to offer information of a general nature to help you in your quest for emotional and spiritual well-being. In the event you use any of the information in this book for yourself, which is your constitutional right, the author and the publisher assume no responsibility for your actions.*

*Any people depicted in stock imagery provided by Thinkstock are models, and such images are being used for illustrative purposes only.*
*Certain stock imagery © Thinkstock.*

*Printed in the United States of America*

*Balboa Press rev. date: 07/03/2012*

"Without Rose I may never have discovered the truth of the Law of Attraction. Her stories of success inspired me to make an attempt at attracting what I needed most. All these are being realised!"
Helen – Hertfordshire

For David and Jackie

Thank you for your loving support over the last years.

# Acknowledgements

This little book has evolved over time—like everything in life. There are several people who contributed in very specific ways, as well as others who constantly encouraged me to put my philosophical thoughts on life into print.

I am particularly grateful for the constant guidance of David: who has done a brilliant job of being my older brother, scolding and encouraging me at the appropriate times. Without his help I'm sure my work would not have got off the ground. I'd like to thank my sister-in-law, Jackie, who has proof-read this work and everything I've written, which has brought me to this point now. I would also like to thank Paul, who, again and again, has kept me on track. No easy task I'm sure, as I am want to wander at times.

I'm very grateful to Vicky for reading the fledgling ideas and the subsequent manuscripts. Vicky, Kathie and Anne have given me encouragement every step of the way. They have all supported me when I took one step back and were delighted when I took two steps forward. Thank you for believing in me. Thank you too, to Judith Mackay for her delightful illustrations.

# An Introduction to the Law of Attraction

It seems like the Law of Attraction is tripping off everyone's lips these days. And so it should be.

The Law of Attraction is a natural Law of the Universe– just like Gravity–and they both work 24/7. We don't wake up in the morning and think to ourselves, 'Oh, I must remember to work with Gravity today to keep my feet on the ground'. Gravity does its job whether we are aware of it or not. The Law of Attraction does its job of creation and manifestation, whether we are aware of it or not.

It is the Law of Creation. Our entire universe was created and is being recreated constantly and continuously by the Law of Attraction. All creation and physical manifestation is as a result of the workings of this Law.

Your life is a reflection of your dance with the Law of Attraction. The Law of Attraction is simple, constant and non-judgemental. You and I and all of mankind are complex and complicated: ever-changing and exceedingly judgemental. In a nutshell, we create our lives by our thoughts and feelings, and by the meaning we give to all our experiences. It is as simple as that.

The tricky part of creating what you want in life is to accept that you do indeed create it all, and then to adjust your thoughts and feelings to bring them into alignment with the energy/vibration of your desire. If you want a different life, then it's you who needs to change, and the Law of Attraction will deliver the goods. Nothing changes until you do.

Learning how to create the life you want is a journey, but not a journey of learning about the Law of Attraction. It is a journey of self-discovery and personal growth, which automatically leads to spiritual growth. This journey is never-ending. Not only will it take this life time, but all our other life times too—because we are recreating ourselves in every moment. There is no completion—ever. There is always more.

It is right that more and more people are becoming aware that they create their own reality and that they create absolutely everything in their lives, including the bits they don't like. The more people that are aware of creating their lives, and consciously choose so to do, the better, happier and more peaceful our world will become.

# Water

Why is it, do you think, that we like to sit by water?

I sit by a lake in the Forest of Dean in western England, gazing out over the calm water. A slight breeze causes tiny ripples. The leaves are beginning to turn golden. Somehow, every year, the beginning of autumn takes me by surprise. It always seems to be early. Perhaps it's because I've not yet finished with summer?

The water is calm and still. I am at peace with myself, with nature and with my God. I find being in a place of natural beauty, especially by water, no matter how big or small, very 'whole-making'. It seems as if I getting in touch with the part of Me that's bigger than the Me I'm aware of on a daily basis. No matter how troubled I am, when I sit or walk by water it quietens my mind and feeds my Soul.

# The Purpose of Life

Have I mentioned that I frequently talk to God? I often say, "God, this is the problem. I know you already know this, but I'm going to tell you anyway". Then I go over the current problem that has my full attention. Then I say words to the effect, "God, you know me so well and you know I'm always in a hurry. I do appreciate that you're very busy at the moment ... but could I please have an answer by 5 o'clock?" I usually get an answer before 5 o'clock!

One morning, I was troubled by something that was deep and profound. I had my 'usual-type' of conversation with God and asked, "Why are we here? What is the purpose of life?" Then I carried on with my housework.

Hours later, soft words started to drift into my mind, rather like smoke drifting lazily though the air. The words were there before I was conscious of thinking them. It was the answer to my questions.

Before we left God, we stood before Him, naked in our innocence. When we return to God, when we've finished on our cycle of birth and death, we will once again stand naked before Him, but this time we will be naked in our wisdom.

And that's the purpose of life.

# Comfort Zone

They say that life begins outside the box: outside your comfort zone. If you think about it, you'll see that 'they' are quite right. If you only live inside your comfort zone, you aren't really living, you are just existing within your limited frame-work.

For us to live a rich, fulfilling and meaningful life we have to expand—we need to grow. We have two options in life—we grow or we die. So, we mostly choose to grow.

We grow until we fill our comfort zone and then we are no longer comfortable. We are then forced to be brave and step outside our box to experience more of life.

Get yourself out of your box. Step across the line and believe in yourself. It's scary, but not doing so really is not an option, is it?

# Talking to Ducks

Mostly, I find talking to ducks very satisfying. They are usually attentive, well sort-of, and appear to listen. However, I'm under no illusions about their loyalty, which is totally dependent on the bread I throw. It really is a cupboard-love relationship.

Talking to ducks is a way of clearing my mind. I can tell them of the merry-go-round of my thoughts and the stuff going on in my life. They make no judgements and don't tell me what to do. I have a good therapeutic, working relationship with ducks.

Once I've emptied my head of the dross I've been carrying around, I can see clearly the questions that need to be asked and then I can answer them.

I always ask myself the important questions of life–as I find that I am the only one who gives me reasonable answers.

# Dichotomies

Do you like puzzles? I do–particularly jigsaw puzzles. Dichotomies are sort-of like Universal puzzles. There are two dichotomies in life (I suppose there are many more, but there are two I'm aware of at this time) regarding the workings of the Law of Attraction. One is that we need the things in life that we don't want, so we can then know the things we do want. The things we don't want are our 'feedback system' of life.

But, instead of recognizing that although life is not offering us what we want, it is giving us the opportunity to decide what we do want and then to create it, we get so caught up with what's in front of us. We get distracted by what is going on around us. We become embroiled in the drama of it. We love drama. We even love to be scared. Think of all the scary movies we watch! We love it all.

It does mean though, that we're focusing on what we don't want, instead of focusing on what we do want–which also means that we are going to get more of what we don't want, again!

The dichotomy? We need the very things we don't like to give us clarity for what we actually do want.

Unfortunately, we become too distracted by the bit we don't want and forget that we can create a path to what we do want, in a snap of our fingers.

And the second dichotomy? I can't remember. I hope I do remember before I get to the end of the book!

# Parking Places

I still get a thrill when I create a parking place exactly where I want it. Do you create parking places? Of course you do. Are you good at it? Of course you are. Do you get a thrill creating a space exactly where you want it, like I do? Of course you do!

Our greatest joy comes from consciously creating what we want in life. You are delighted and thrilled when you deliberately create a parking place!

Imagine the absolute thrill and excitement you will feel when you create something really important in life!

That is Joy.

That is Freedom!

That's what life's all about!

# Clouds

How long is it since you lay on the grass watching the clouds change and shape-shift into things of your imagination? Too long, perhaps?

The clouds change shape as quickly as our reality changes. We do create our own reality, moment by moment, albeit that most people have no idea that they do so. But you do know this otherwise you would not have picked up this book. Yes, although you might push it to the back-burner or forget it sometimes, you do know you create your own life, don't you?

Instead of enjoying the twists and turns we have created to make our life interesting, we become trapped in what we've already created without realizing it. We forget we've created it and that we can create something else just as easily and as quickly as the wind changes the shapes in the clouds.

Look up into the sky and see a world of possibilities.

# Air, Water, Earth and Fire

Which Element do you feel an affinity with: Air, Water, Earth or Fire?

I am an Air person. I love the wind. Joy and Freedom is standing on top of a cliff, looking at the distant horizon, circling through 360 degrees and seeing nothing but wide open space. Now, add the wind–I don't care how strong it is! I just love it.

I'm sure you know what type of person you are. You'll know if you are 'Watery' or love to dig your hands into the Earth, or just love to feel the heat of the Sun on your skin best of all.

In your creative visualisations, use your imagination to bring in your Element–in its power! The force of the Wind: the might of the Sea: the depth of the Earth or the heat of the Sun can be used to increase your feelings in your meditation. And, as you know, the more intense your emotions, the sooner your creations come back to you.

# **Mountains**

Have I mentioned that I love mountains? In all the countries I've lived and travelled to, I have met some really amazing mountains and I have gathered a few 'very favourite ones'. I like mountains.

The bow of the ship cut through the dark sea smoothly and silently. The silence hung heavily in the air, as did the mist, as we sailed into the fiord. I was up at dawn, (have I mentioned that I love the dawn?) I was up at dawn, standing on the bow of the ship, enjoying this most spectacular site. I was spell-bound. Such breath-taking beauty!

The mountains on either side seemed to close in. They were colossal faces of black rock–cold, silent and unforgiving. The sea, which carried the reflection of the mountains, also looked black, cold–and so deep.

There was no sign of the sun and in the dull grey light of dawn the mist seemed to hang, suspended over the small town at the end of the fiord.

The silence was eerie. The magnificence: the majesty: the might of the mountains moved me. I was awed by their power. Their beauty was breath-taking.

Do you know that you have the same magnificent and majestic power within you? It's inherent within every one of us. And we don't have to earn it; it's there for us to use.

All we have to do is to use it is acknowledge it. Choice is your power. Make choices and decisions on how you would like your life to be! Make a choice now! You have the power to do so and, in fact, you are the only one that can make choices for your life.

(I recommend listening to 'In the Hall of the Mountain King' by Grieg whilst reading this. Play it loud–the neighbours will love it too!)

# Air Power

The lure of the view from the top of the lighthouse was irresistible. That's saying something, as I'm afraid of heights. I'm not afraid of going up, but I find coming down absolutely terrifying. But, am I going to let my fear stop me going to the top of the lighthouse? You're right, I'm not! The view from the top: the promise of seeing a 180 degree view of the ocean: the feeling of a strong wind blowing: was calling me.

So, up the lighthouse I went–well half-way up anyway– before the panic about getting down overwhelmed me. So, I did what anyone in these circumstances would do– I immediately sat down on the narrow step, holding the bannister very tightly, eyes closed.

Fear is valid. There is nothing wrong with fear. It stops us walking off the edge of cliffs. The way to deal with it is to step into it, feel the fear–and then do it anyway, as the saying goes (but not if you're near the edge of a cliff).

So I thought about the view from the top and the wind (have I mentioned that I love the wind?) and began to climb again.

Before the lighthouse-keeper opened the door at the top, he warned about the strength of the wind and told us to immediately grab hold of the railing! I stepped out onto the narrow ledge and was greeted enthusiastically by the wind! It rushed around me excitedly. It was very pleased to see me, and I it. The view from the top of the lighthouse was every bit as stunning as I knew it would be. It was beautiful out there on the ledge and the wind was wonderful. It was exhilarating and so very good for my Soul.

How did I get down? Slowly: very slowly indeed and one step at a time. But I was so excited and thrilled–it could be said that I was 'as high as a kite'. I had overcome one of my main fears, I had seen a spectacular view of the ocean and I have wonderful memories.

## Conscious Creation

When I first heard that I 'created my own reality' I was thrilled. It seemed a wonderful concept and it meant that I could have whatever I wanted, just by thinking about it. At that time, I didn't think much beyond adding more 'stuff' to my life: having more 'toys' to play with.

We create everything in our lives by the Law of Attraction, (for that is what reality creation is now called). This is based on the principle of Like attracts Like and as you can imagine, not all of my creations manifested as I wanted. I had some dismal failures.

So I started to find out more about this natural Law so that I could have the life of my dreams. But I found that learning how the Law of Attraction works isn't all that's required to creating a successful life.

I found that our lives are a reflection of our own dance with the Law of Attraction. The Law of Attraction is simple, constant and non-judgemental.

We, as human beings, are just the opposite. We are complex and complicated: changeable and extremely judgemental.

It takes only a short while to learn about the Law of Attraction, but it takes a lifetime to learn about ourselves. Consciously creating success in your life starts with self-awareness and self-knowledge. A happy and successful life begins with 'Man-Know Thyself.

# The Past is a Present

That sounds almost as if it's a trick, doesn't it? When I first heard that phrase, I thought it meant that the past is in the present and I thought, "Yes–that's right. A lot of people keep their past alive in their present". The past is not a place it is an attitude of life. Many people live their 'past' every day and they even throw their attitude of the past forward into tomorrow, too.

Then I thought about its real meaning and this, too, is true. Whatever happened in the past, whether you liked it or not, whether you enjoyed it or not, it has brought you to the place you are now–today.

The past shows you what has and hasn't worked. Your past shows you where you can make changes, now in the present, to give you a happier and more fulfilling life. Your past gives you the opportunity to choose something different; to choose something more for your life–today, in this present moment.

I think that the past is definitely a present! Life is a wonderful gift.

# Signposts

Do you ever wonder if you are on the 'right' path in life? Do you ever ask, 'What is my purpose in life?'

It's so difficult to know the 'right thing' to do. It's almost as if we should have a well-defined 'mission statement'—perhaps a 20 page memorandum, laying out what we should do with our lives and how to do it.

It's easier than that. When you are doing something you love, when you are so completely absorbed in what you're doing that time stands still, you can rest assured you're doing what you are supposed to be doing.

It may seem that it is not possible to make a living by doing what you love to do. However, if you focus on the solution and not the problem, you will find that a way will open up for you to do what you love to do and make to an income in the process.

Know that, at every turn, you will always been shown the next step. There is always a signpost of some description. It might be a few words in a song, or an advertisement—something will come to your mind that is so obvious you cannot think why you didn't realise it earlier.

Do what you love to do and the world will come to you.

# Like a Tea Bag

Do you know that each day, in so many ordinary ways, you touch your Soul? Or rather, you allow your Soul to touch you.

We have far more 'spiritual experiences' a day than we realise. It's those times when we go fuzzy round the edges, as if our boundaries blur and we seem to blend into life. This can happen in a myriad of ways; from walking in nature, looking at a landscape (that does it for me, every time); sitting with your beloved pet; cooking; gardening; or to listening music. So many things can put us in these diffused states when we are completely happy and content; where truly all is well with our world.

At these times, it seems as if we are permeable and the love and pleasure of life just flows into us and through us. It's a bit like being a tea bag, isn't it?

## **Stepping Stones**

The path wandered beside a fast–flowing stream. The sunlight danced on the water as it rushed along to its destination and it looked as if it had been sprinkled with diamonds.

There was a crossing place–stepping stones. One or two of the stones were a natural part of the stream and some had been strategically placed to make crossing easier.

'Easier' being a relative term. Some of the stones were sharp and some wobbly. It required concentration to maintain balance so that you didn't slip into water. The stream wasn't deep, but it was wet–and probably cold too! Sometimes the distance between stones was short, but taking that step could be hazardous.

Life is a string of stepping stones. Even though you might be on a wobbly stone that is causing you anxiety and worry, this stone is showing you the way to the next stone ahead.

You may not like where you are, but being where you are is the only way to get to where you want to be.

Life is a series of stepping stones. Life flows through us, drawing us forward. There is always more and we'll never get it done!

## Sea Shells

Have you been to the beach lately? Do you take a bag to collect shells? I do.

When I lived in Dubai I loved walking along the shore looking for shells. Sometimes I'd walk along the high tide mark, but mostly, I walked in and out of the waves–through the foamy bits that run up the sand and then rushed back into the sea again.

I collected seashells, and no matter how many I had, I always picked up more. I chose the ones that caught my eye, glinting in the sun or the shells that seemed to have a particular depth of colour, mainly because they were still wet. I'd pick one up, look at it and turn it over to get the 'feel' of it. Was this the right one for me? If it wasn't I'd return it from whence it came. If it was I'd pop it into my bag and walk on, scanning the sand for another gem.

However, and I'm sure this has happened to you, too, I ended up with so many shells, most of them looking and feeling the same, and the collection just seemed to grow and grow. None of them meant anything to me any longer, but I kept them anyway.

Your life is your collection of seashells. We wander through life, looking at various incidents and experiences in life, and we decide whether we would like to benefit from them or not. The problem is that we get so involved in the collection of the seashells that it weighs us down: it traps us and doesn't leave us free to go wandering along the beach again.

Have you noticed the greatest pleasure is in the wandering and selecting the shells, not in the having and keeping them? It's the journey that brings us joy—not reaching the destination.

# Who Are You?

You are goodness, mercy and compassion
You are understanding, peace, joy and light
You are forgiveness, patience, wisdom and grace
You are gentleness, courage, and a star shining bright.

You are kindness, gratitude and appreciation
You are humility, harmony, respect, hope and love
You are well-being and abundance, freedom and faith
You are Spiritual and at One with God above.

## Walking in Treacle

Recently I've encountered a phrase ... 'I feel as if I'm walking through treacle'. A flash came to my mind of me being 'knee-deep' in treacle. As I'm not particularly fond of the taste or the smell of treacle, I find the thought of trying just to lift one foot, let alone having to push myself forward through the sticky goo, more than a bit frightening.

We often feel as if we are standing in treacle and can't get out of it! We give all our attention to the treacle, instead of considering making treacle pudding!

Today forget the treacle and remember the pudding!

Focus on smiles rather than frowns: possibilities rather than problems.

# Friendship

We sat together, my friend and I
Chatting over biscuits and tea.
We talked together of this and that,
Of her, our families and me.

Together we sat, my friend and I
Talking over supper and wine.
We talked and laughed, laughed some more
Not conscious of the time.

The Law of Attraction watched us play
And sent us more ten-fold.
We loved and laughed, laughed and loved
Our friendship, as rich as gold.

*For Kathie and Vicky*

# Begin Where You Are

I think I've mentioned (probably several times) that you can only begin where you are. This may seem an obvious statement and yet so many are not aware of it, or not even aware of where, in fact, they are.

If you try to start from somewhere else, you will not achieve what you are trying to achieve. You are where you are and you need to recognise it and be comfortable with it before you can move on. While you are upset or irritable about something you are creating more of it. What you resist; persists.

The point of attraction for the Law of Attraction is Now. You are creating more of what you are feeling Now–in this instant. If you don't want more of the same, change the meaning you've given to the experience. Change the meaning and you'll change the feeling.

# Dreams and Visions

You do have dreams don't you? You do dream of a better life and of having more than you have now? Oh, I hope you do!

Your dreams are your reason to grow. Your dreams are your inspiration to become more than you are today. Without your dreams you have nothing pulling you forward; no feelings of accomplishment and achievement; no feelings of joy for a successful creation. Without dreams there would be no Hope–and how sad that would be!

Your life is about your dreams. You need them to create a better life. More importantly–the world needs your dreams! Dream on.

# Thank You

I'm sure as a young child you were taught to write Thank You letters for the gifts you received for your birthday and at Christmas time. Although the letters were possibly written under duress, after all it's quite difficult to write enthusiastically about receiving another pair of socks, the letters were expression of appreciation and gratitude.

The principle is exactly on track with the workings of the Law of Attraction. If you have something in your life that delights you, write a thank you letter to the Universe. List all the things about your situation that you appreciate and for which you are grateful.

Feelings of gratitude and appreciation open doors you didn't even know were there-like magic!

## **<u>Oh, and Another Thing</u>**

And another thing … You can't have a happy holiday if you have an unhappy journey travelling there.

It's the same as life and the Law of Attraction. If you don't like how you are feeling (the journey) you will not like what the Universe delivers (the holiday).

Every thought is creative. Every feeling is creative. The Universe will always deliver more of what you are feeling. Your feelings are laying the path, taking you to where you are going. Wouldn't you like to be pleased with life when you get there? I thought you would.

Well then, be pleased, delighted and happy with the journey of getting there. Be pleased with your day–every day. And not only will you enjoy each day but you'll enjoy the future when it becomes your present too.

# Three Gorgeous Girls

Once upon a time (all good fairy tales begin with Once upon a time) so—as I said, once upon a time there were two beloved sisters, who were renowned for their beauty. They lived in a wonderful castle in a far-off country with an unpronounceable name. One of these beauties was called Snow White for, indeed, her skin was as fair as the driven snow. Snow White liked to walk in the woods and so gentle and kind was she that she very soon made friends with the animals and birds of the forest.

The other child liked to stitch and spin, and could be found sitting at her spinning-wheel by the window, day after day. However, she was inclined to fall asleep at her wheel and hence became known as Sleeping Beauty.

There is a third girl in our story. She was a servant girl who lived 'below stairs' and worked in the kitchen. Her job was to clean out the ash and cinders from the large fire-place and so it came to pass that she was called Cinderella.

Each of these girls went through their own particular initiation of life. Snow White choked on an apple and went into a coma: Sleeping Beauty pricked her finger and fell asleep for a hundred years. (I'm not sure about the logistics of this, but I'm going to go with it for the sake of the story), and Cinderella who, as the story goes, had a fairy godmother (wouldn't we all like one of those) who had a Harry Potter wand (wouldn't we all like one of *those?*). She sprinkled

Cinderella with fairy-dust to create a beautiful ball gown; turned Snow White's mice into horses; turned a pumpkin into a coach and so Cinderella went to the ball in grand style to meet her prince.

You know the end of each the story. Snow White's prince trudged through a forest to find his Love in a glass coffin. When he kissed her tenderly to awaken her, she started coughing violently and dislodged the offending piece of apple! Sleeping Beauty's prince hacked his way through hundred years' worth of thick briars, to climb to the ivory town to rescue his beautiful princess. While Prince Charming only had to retrieve a lost shoe (surely this is the easiest of all the tasks?).

The moral of the story is that each one of us is Snow White, Sleeping Beauty and Cinderella, as these stories all have the same meaning, which is about us becoming connected with the True Love of our Soul and to the true, unconditional Love of the Devine.

# The Next Step

A long time ago (but not that long ago that I can't remember), my daughter, then aged about 12, and I were driving along a long, straight road–the sort of long, straight road you can only get in big, spacious countries, where the road seems to go on and on for ever, without any signs of 'getting there'.

It seemed as if the gentle curve of the horizon was so far away in distance that we would never get there.

Suddenly my daughter said, 'I know why the earth is round and we can't see beyond the horizon. It's because, if we could see too far down the road, we might be too afraid to go there'.

We don't need to see too far down the road at all. We only need to be able to see enough to take the next step.

## Give It Some Heart

There is a television car advertisement which shows a very shapely lady, in her very high heels getting out of a similarly shapely car – and the tag line is, *'Without heart we are only machines'*.

And I thought how true! None of us wants to be like a machine. Life would be so dull without emotions! Put your heart into everything you do.

Throw your heart over the bar first today and the rest of you will follow.

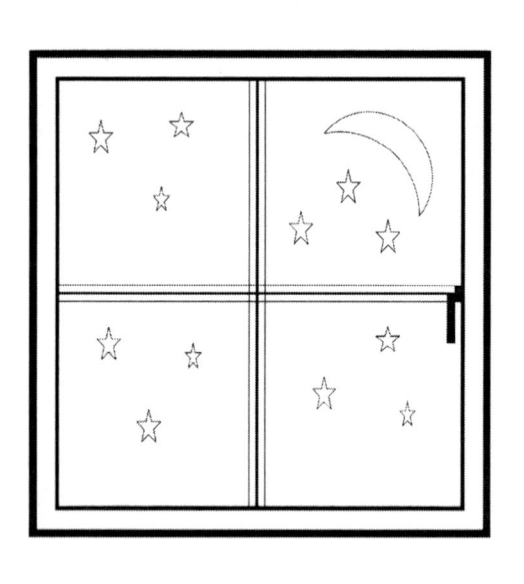

# Magic Window

It's nearly Christmas and the snow is falling. In fact it's been snowing for over a week now. It's definitely hot chocolate weather. I wonder if it will be a White Christmas this year. Wouldn't that be enchanting?

I love Christmas. On a recent television programme, someone mentioned a 'magic window' and I thought, 'That's what Christmas is for young children'. There is a sparkle and enchantment about Christmas for youngsters particularly. They not only believe, but they know that magic and miracles are part of life.

Children look at Christmas through a 'magic window' where everything is possible. They send out their dreams and the 'Law of Attraction' in the form of a large, fat man in a red suit with a jelly-bean hat, comes down the chimney to deliver their wishes under the sparkling Christmas tree, all wrapped with pretty paper and ribbons. Pure magic.

And life is wonderful when you consciously work with the Law of Attraction; you can look through the 'magic window' of your imagination to create the dreams and wishes you have for your life. You can dream, imagine everything you want into being. See and feel the excitement and thrill of a child as you create what you want. Then, either let your dreams drift away like bubbles, or hold the resonance of excited anticipation until they are delivered to you – maybe even before $25^{th}$ December.

The world needs of your dreams. Dream dreams for yourself: dream dreams for those you love and dream dreams for your world and send them off, with hope and love.

## Love and Buttered Toast

While I was chopping carrots the other day, listening to the radio, I heard a song about a man who was searching for a very special love; a love that could 'turn bread into buttered toast'. I think being able to turn the ordinary 'staff of life' into something so deliciously yummy as buttered toast, is alchemy. This type of alchemy needs the magic of a very special kind of love. It's the kind of love we all dream about.

To find this magical love, call on the Law of Attraction. Work your alchemy by adding love and happiness to your own life. Remember: Like attracts Like. So, if you want to attract buttered toast, first you must become buttered toast.

# Which Path?

There comes a time in life when one definitely needs tea to help with pondering—and perhaps even a biscuit might be required, if the situation is challenging. This is just such a time.

I have a conundrum.

Have you ever been very sure of where you are going and have been happily travelling along that path with a destination in sight, albeit far down the road, only to find out you've actually been a few degrees off course and that another destination is possibly the 'right' destination, after all?

Today, I realised that I had possibly been a few degrees off my mark. Now I've realised this, it all seems so very obvious. 'How did I miss it in the first place?' I ask myself? (I always ask myself the important questions in life, as I've found that I am the only one that gives me reasonable answers!)

I started to think. Were there two paths available to me in the first place? Or, did the second path only come into being as a result of the first? These are tough questions indeed and tea and biscuits definitely help to solve the mystery.

Now I'm sure. The second path only came into being as a result of the first. It was sort of 'shadowing' the first. Without the first path, I might never have seen a second one, which now has the possibility of being the 'more-true' path—at this time.

So, in effect, the first path was not the 'wrong' path. It was absolutely essential in order for the second path to come into being.

*This and That*

So, when you are a little unsure of where you are heading, make tea and look closely at what you're doing, and then look in its shadow and you might be surprised by what you see. Things are often under our noses, but we don't notice.

# The Beatles and Elvis

However, not all things in life are so deep and meaningful that they require tea and biscuits to help with pondering. What has come to mind today certainly isn't. It's light and frothy, a bit like cappuccino.

The other day, while doing some serious work, I had a Beatles CD playing on the stereo–loud, of course. Now, I bet you are thinking that I'm going to write about music and vibrations and how we have to align our vibrations with what we want. Well, I wasn't, but I can if you like–but perhaps another time.

It was just that I had a very nifty thought! Their song 'No Reply' was playing and I thought–'they've got it all wrong!' The Law of Attraction always replies. There is always a 'reply' to every thought we think.

And I realised that Elvis has got it right with 'Return to Sender'. That's what the Law of Attraction does.

# Musings on Elephants and other Big Stuff

This story can't really be classified as belonging to one particular branch of philosophy. It's what I'd call Everyday Philosophy, but it's important, none the less.

There are times when it seems as if life is rushing past us. We seem to get lost in swirls of frantic energy and feel as if we cannot cope. At times like these, the best way to get some perspective on life is to ask yourself, 'How do you eat an elephant?'

Do you know how to eat an elephant—you eat it a bite at a time. You move a sand dune one shovel at a time. You build a house one brick at a time.

Chunk down the stresses in your life: make them into small bites. Clump them down in groups of three. Do you know that a baboon can count up to three? So, if an ape can cope with three things, surely we can too. You will be able to look at life more calmly when it is in small chunks, as it is easier to prioritize and regain control. Life is easier to digest in smaller chunks.

And that's how you eat an elephant, the same way you live life: slowly, a bite at a time, savouring each morsel.

# Musings on Pooh Bear

I've always felt that the writings of A A Milne are wasted on the young. It seems to me that the true philosophy of this work only becomes apparent as we mature.

Consider the pastime playing Pooh Sticks. This is a seemingly mindless game for a lazy summer's day. If you are unfamiliar with this game, you need to find yourself a convenient river (preferably one as lazy as your summer day) with a bridge. Then you gather small twigs and, looking up-stream, hang over the side of the bridge, drop the sticks into the river and watch them slowly drifting under the bridge.

If you are playing with a friend, then the child in you will run to the other side of the bridge to see whose stick came through first. And then, of course, you run back to play the next round.

If you were to imagine that every stick you drop is one of your troubles, you can watch your woes disappearing from your life as they slowly slip under the bridge. You can just let your troubles float away with the river.

A word of warning; keep a tight rein on 'the child within'. Don't let it go running to watch your troubles reappearing on the other side, as this negates the therapeutic effect of playing Pooh Sticks.

# Look Where You're Going

Life can be so confusing. While we were growing up we were told to look where we are going. This is vital advice– apart from being handy so that we don't walk into lamp-posts –but do you realise that your whole life is the result of looking where you're going?

How many times have you said to yourself, 'I knew that was going to happen–I just knew that so and so was going to happen!' So and so happened because you were focusing on that situation. You imagined that situation happening.

The Law of Attraction and the Universe will always deliver what you focus on.

Notice where you put your attention and, if you don't want to go there, focus on the place you really want to be.

# <u>Change</u>

Isn't it amazing how many of us wish we could change the world in some way or another? I don't mean the philanthropic dreams we all have of how we could change so many lives when we win the jackpot in the lottery. I mean, how we wish we could change something about our parents, our spouse, our children, the boss, a colleague or any number of the people we come into contact with every day.

When you understand the workings of the Law of Attraction and you know that you attract things to yourself with your thoughts and feeling, then it must be so for everyone else too.

You will know that you cannot create something for another or change the life of another. You'll also know that you have no control over external circumstances either.

Understanding the Law of Attraction means that you know you cannot change anything outside of yourself: you know that if you want life to change, you have to change.

**Nothing changes until you do.**

## Meaning and Purpose

Do you sometimes feel as if your life has no purpose? Do you feel as if you're on a hamster-wheel doing the same old monotonous things; day after day.

Everyone needs a sense of significance and purpose. We all need to have a reason to get out of bed in the morning. Some spend lifetimes looking for their specific purpose–but there's no predestined purpose for us to fulfill in life.

It's much niftier than being given something specific to do with your life: you can choose what gives your life meaning. You can choose the purpose you give life.

However it isn't like throwing a dart at the dart-board: you have very strong clues as where to go and what to do with your life. Do what you love to do; do what you get lost in; do what makes your heart sing–it's a worn-out saying, but it still says it all.

Life has no purpose, save the one you give it. Tell the Universe your truth and it will deliver an exceptional life! To succeed in life, you have to believe in something with such a passion that it becomes a reality.

# The Wind of Change

A long time ago, I lived in a far-off land in the middle of Africa that was involved in a bitter and cruel terrorist war. My husband was part of the armed forces and was away for extended periods of time. And I had two young children.

Life was fraught with the stress of the political situation. The war had a major impact on our daily lives. Our safety was constantly under threat, even in the cities, and there were shortages of essential food and fuel supplies. And there were the normal stresses of motherhood.

I just wanted to feel better. I wanted to feel as if I could cope with each day without being irritable and intolerant with the children, as a result of continuous anxiety and strain. Oh, how I wanted so much, just to feel better.

*"The wind of change is blowing through the African continent...."* and indeed that 'wind' did change many things in our land and in other lands too. But it also brought an important change to me. I realized that although I could not change the political situation, I could change the direction of my thoughts and feelings. In fact, it was the only thing I could change. I could and indeed did, find a way to feel better!*

*"The wind of change is blowing through this (African) continent, and whether we like it or not, this growth of national consciousness is a political fact."*
*Sir Harold MacMillan. Cape Town. 3rd February 1960*
*Bach Flower Remedies

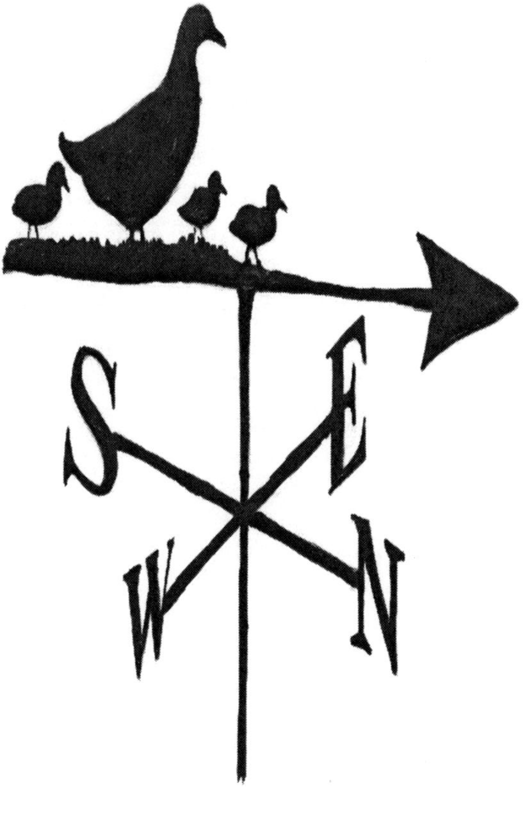

S
E
W
N

# **Ten Minute Difference**

There is a short period of time between awakening from sleep and coming into full conscious awareness. It's that luxurious time when you are still relaxed from sleep, calm and dozy, before the cogs of your mind become fully engaged.

One of my favourite things is to lie there, savouring my slow awakening to the day. I find that a gentle calmness flows softly into my consciousness and I then take ten minutes to think about my day. The first choice of the day is always that today will be a happy and successful day, and that only good things will come to me.

It only takes ten minutes to set the tone for the whole day.

# A Very Special Friendship

*Dear Vicky*

I don't know when the seed of our friendship was planted. I'm sure it had germinated and was sprouting before we realised it was growing.

Over the years it has grown to be something most caring and beautiful: deep and rich. I don't think I could identify all the different ways we have come to know and love each other. It feels natural: as if it's always been. It seems to come from the depths of our Souls.

Our personal dreams and global visions for a better life for all, add to the wonder of our friendship.

If we haven't known each other in other life-times, then we are now laying a beautiful foundation for life-times to come. What joy!

# Inside Job

When my mind is chaotic, churning around with too many things I don't know what to do about, and too many things that need to be done that I don't know how to do, I begin to tidy up. It's at times like these that I like everything to be clean and tidy and in its right place –sometimes I become extremely fastidious.

I have found the more chaos there is inside my mind, the more I need to control my surroundings: be in control of what is 'outside' of me.

When I become aware that I'm being frantically tidy, I know that it has nothing to do with what is going on around me–it's all an Inside Job.

So I stop, make tea and then begin to put my mind in order. I make priority lists: find a way of doing the most urgent and important things, look for logical explanations to worries and generally calm my mind. And as if by magic, my outside world follows suit.

When your outside world troubles you, take a deep breath and realise there is nothing to be done to change life–it's all an Inside Job!

## Law of Attraction

There is a continuous flow of Consciousness that is Universal Energy. This energy has many names: Source Energy: Universal Force Field and God/Goddess/All That Is, to mention a few. It is also referred to by some as the Universal Mind of God.

The Universal Mind is un-manifested energy. It's the substance out of which all physical things are made. Can you imagine an infinite lump of clay that you can mould and shape into anything you want? The Universal Force Field is such a lump of clay. Source Energy is available for us to sculpt and carve it into whatever physical form we like.

We are part of the Universal Mind. All That Is is perfection and creates our lives in accordance with our thoughts and feelings; our beliefs and attitudes. Our inner picture of the world is reproduced perfectly.

We can learn how the Universal Mind works and we can create unlimited abundance, health and well-being and greater happiness. It always creates every detail we think and feel.

The method by which our thoughts and feelings become our physical world is now called the Law of Attraction. It can also be called Cause and Effect.

# You've got the Music in You.

I think that some song writers are really quite perceptive. Right now, there is someone on the radio beating out a hearty rhythm and telling me that I have the music in me. He is quite right. We all have our own particular music: we sing our own song: we all dance to our own rhythm.

We find it easy to understand that music is a vibration. You may not hear your music in the same way as I can hear the song from the radio, but we do create our own unique vibration with our thoughts and feelings.

We have our own distinctive tone and even our tone of voice is an expression of the music that is within us.

# Glow Worms

I was told the other day that Winston Churchill said "We are all worms–but I'm a glow-worm".

I rather care for this. If I must be a worm; I would rather be a special worm, wouldn't you? So, I think I'll be a Glow-Worm too.

Do you think that glow-worms could turn into glowing butterflies? This is food for thought indeed because, as we know, if we have the where-withal to imagine something, then the Universe has the where-withal to create it.

Keep your eyes peeled for glowing butterflies, please.

# Tea in Bed

I find there is something particularly luxurious about having tea in bed in the mornings and, although I take my tea to bed every morning, I still revel in it. It is my 'thinking' time when I write my thoughts of yesterday and my plans for today. This is also my inspirational reading time as I set myself up for the day. Even if I have an early start, I'll wake early enough to have my tea-in-bed time.

You know that your feelings create your life. You know the power of positive thoughts. How do you know—because you've experienced both? But, do you realise that every thought you think is creating something in your life: it's just as if you're laying a paving stone in the pathway to where you're going.

My tea-in-bed time is the time when I lay the paving stones to my future.

# Buttons, Cages and Boats

Did you think you'd go through life without anyone pushing your buttons or rattling your cage? Did you think you get through your proverbial Six Score Years and Ten without someone rocking your boat?

If you did, then you're imagining life as a Disneyland fantasy: pure whimsy—and you would be bored before Wednesday.

Cage-rattling, button-pushing and boat-rocking, irritating though they may be, indicate there are great opportunities for increased growth looking you in the face. Life is your feed-back system letting you know you have a choice to change things. The choice is always yours.

# The Alpha and the Omega.

I'm sure you know about Alpha and Omega.

Well, I was thinking about beginnings and endings (as, of course, one often does). I like the beginning and the ending of the day.

The dawn and sunrise are very special times for me and I'm not sure why. It's as if the sun's fingers of pink and mauve say, "Here is the Light of a brand new day". And that beautiful time at the end of the day as the sun sinks slowly beneath the horizon and we enter the "twilight zone"–the time of magic and miracles–that the sun is saying "Goodnight. Sleep well rested".

If you start the beginning of your day with loving thoughts, you'll have a loving day. If you have a loving day, you'll end the day with loving thoughts. For, after all, Love is all there is–Love is The Alpha and The Omega.

# Gran'ma's Principle

My mother was a wonderful and wise lady. Her favourite book was 'The Power of Positive Thinking' by Norman Vincent Peale and so we were brought up on a diet rich in positive thought.

When we did something that didn't turn out quite the way we expected, my mother used to say: "Never mind. It may not be good–but it's better than it was."

This piece of wisdom was naturally handed down to my children when they had to deal with disappointment and so, it soon became known as 'Gran'ma's Principle', which is still very much a part of my daily philosophy on life.

# Look after the Pennies

We get ourselves into such a muddle worrying about the big things in life that we seem to pass over the little things.

Have you ever noticed that when you don't tend to the little things, perhaps around the house, at the office or in the garden, that they tend to clump together and suddenly they are a big thing that needs attention **now!** It always seems to me that my heap of ironing seems to have a mind of its own–it seems to grow when I'm not looking and then it takes me hours to clear it.

I love the philosophy of life. Joy is not found in the big things that come every now and then. Our happiness is found in the little things, which then clump together and create big things which bring us great joy.

I think I now understand the true meaning of the saying, "Look after the pennies and the pounds will look after themselves".

# The Bear and the Tortoise

I have a saying that I use a lot: 'Life Happens'. It seems to cover all the things that don't fit into a previous labelled 'shoe box'. It's when, somehow, despite our best efforts, using all the tricks of our trade, visualisations and happy, positive thoughts, our goals don't seem to come to pass!

There are times when 'life happens' and it isn't always possible for me to see the good things. Now is such a time. This is hard going when, not only is it what I teach, but it is what I live on a daily basis too. I tried various ways to turn my thoughts this way and that, but they kept on slipping back into 'nothing much'–and this is how I went about my days: thinking and doing, nothing much.

But, I have at last found a way. I decided to consider the past weeks a bit like an emotional 'hibernation'. Bears and tortoises go into hibernation in winter. They eat themselves silly at the end of summer and at the beginning of autumn. I'd already started that! Then they find somewhere nice 'n' dry to roll up into a ball and sleep until spring. The tortoise, of course, withdraws entirely into his own shell. It seemed as if I was doing this too. It seems to me that possibly bears and tortoises are the most sensible creatures on the planet!

Withdrawing into one's self can be a very therapeutic process. It is a process of raking over the past, sorting through the jetsam and flotsam of life, looking for the sparkling gems and pearls of wisdom that are lying there, waiting to be collected.

When spring comes we have our beautiful treasure of gems and pearls, which are a part of our Soul we'd forgotten about.

## Say 'Yes'

I've received a greetings card with a photograph of a soft toy–a rabbit–standing on its head, with its ears splayed for balance. He looks really cute and looks as if he's enjoying his play as he views his world upside-down. Young children are inclined to look at the world upside-down sometimes too, aren't they?

I think this might be quite a good thing to do occasionally. We get so caught up and can be quite rigid in the way we look at life, that sometimes a completely upside- down view might just be what we need to bring great changes into our lives.

Today: trying looking at life 'upside-down'. If you don't feel able to do a yoga head-stand or bend in half and look through your legs as you did as a child, then simply say 'Yes' to everything all day and see how life changes.

# The Four 'C's

There's no limit to what you can achieve when you know the secrets of making your dreams come true. When you use the four 'C's you can live your dreams.

**Curiosity** is an absolutely essential part of a happy and successful life. We need to be inquisitive about life and how we interact with it. **Confidence** –*"If one advances confidently in the direction of his dreams, and endeavours to live the life which he has imagined, he will meet with a success unexpected in common hours." Thoreau.* In simple words– "you've done good!" **Courage** –so many of us lack courage to do what we want to do in life. To achieve your dreams, you've got to constantly live outside your comfort zone, and this takes courage. **Consistency**–only constant, consistent perseverance will take you there.

All these qualities stand alone, but mix them together in your own individual way and you'll be unstoppable!

# Sands of Time

You find me sitting on the top of one of the red dunes on the Dubai-Muscat road. They really are very red and quite a different colour to the 'normal' desert-sand that surrounds them. The sun is just setting and, although it's autumn time, it's still hot.

A soft wind is playing with the sand. It twists and swirls and then slithers along the dune and settles again. The wind is not strong enough for the sand to sting. It's a light, refreshing breeze, even though the air is hot. There's a calmness; a serenity about the desert.

We all love to watch water, possibly because it flows and changes as quickly as our emotions. The sand shifts and moves, changing the face of the dunes. There is a saying about 'the shifting sands of time'. Time does move on, shifting and changing the face of our lives too.

Sometimes we don't like where we are and there seems to be too many difficulties, too many reasons why we can't change our lives.

However, if we don't create reasons to change, the shifting sands that change our life will always be in the future and we will never actually live our dreams—which would be a great pity!

# Change

Everything changes and grows constantly. If we stayed as infants it would be really odd and there would no point to life. We've grown to be as old as we are now and by next year we'll all be another year older. Some things are inevitable. We changed from our childish ways (hopefully) and left behind our adolescence attitudes (again, hopefully–otherwise we'd be very difficult to live with) and became the age we are and the person we are today.

Change and growth is vital to all life.

Yet we hate change. I used to go to the hairdresser and say, "I want a new hair style, but as long as I look the same, I'll be fine"! We all need change. There is diversity and variety in life that offers us exciting changes. Our need for growth constantly pulls us forward.

Change is inevitable–except from a vending machine when you need it!

# Ducks in a Row

I think we need to prioritise in life. When we have all our ducks are in a row things seem to fall into place easily. When we prioritise what's important to us, it brings clarity and we are then able to apply laser-like focus to our top priority.

Right now, my top priority is to watch the final of the World Cup Rugby. Or, I could say that my top priority is the heap of ironing that seems to be growing daily. So, I'm off to do the ironing and I may as well watch the rugby at the same time!

I think that is a pretty good deal as it covers two priorities at once. I'm sure you can work out which one is getting my laser-like focus. But both will be done and that will be the first 'two ducks' crossed off my list!

# Stuff and Clutter

Have you got a cupboard under the stairs that's overflowing with 'stuff' that you're keeping, not particularly because you want it, but mainly because you don't want to throw it away? If you don't have such a cupboard, then I know you have a loft that's full of 'stuff'!

Why do we hold on to the stuff of the past? We are weighed down, anchored by the hurt and anger we carry with us from the past. You may not realise it, but the past is not a place—it's an attitude we keep with us daily. But does all the stuff we keep give us a sense of security, perhaps?

The paraphernalia of the past not only limits what we can create today, but it restricts our dreams for the future.

If you want to become aware of the higher good that is happening in your life, be willing to let go of your limited perspective from the past. Clear out the stuff and clutter in the cupboard and loft, and you'll be letting go of some of what limits and restricts you.

**Warning** While clearing out, do not start reminiscing, otherwise you'll put all the stuff and clutter back into the cupboard again—and that defeats the whole object.

## You can–you know

Yesterday, I had to make a major decision. It would take me closer to my dream, but would move me seriously outside of my comfort zone–and you know how scary it is to move out of your comfort zone! I made the decision to go with the dream, rather than just pushing half-heartedly at the side of my box.

But, even this morning, I was not entirely 'settled' with the decision.

I opened one of my favourite books (Think and Grow Rich by Napoleon Hill), seeking solace and inspiration.

The book fell open on page 89. And I quote–because it says it all.

*This and That*

"If you *think* you are beaten, you are,
If you *think* you dare not, you don't
If you like to win, but *think* you can't
It is almost certain you won't.
"If you *think* you'll lose, you're lost
For out of the world we find
Success begins with a fellow's will–
It's all in the *state of mind*.
"If you *think* you are outclassed, you are
You've got to *think* high to rise,
You've got to *be sure of yourself* before
You can ever win a prize.
"Life's battles don't always go
To the stronger or faster man,
But soon or later the man who wins
Is the man *who thinks he can*."

Unknown author. Emphasis is Napoleon Hill's.

# Being Alive

I'm alive and I'm aware of who I am! Today is such a beautiful day and I thank God with every breath I take.

At the moment, Frank Sinatra is inviting me to "come fly" with him. Although the idea of flying away with Ol' Blue Eyes is alluring–I'm not quite sure how or to where we would fly. So think I'll wait for a more practical invitation.

But the music is jolly and matches my aliveness: it matches my delight and my appreciation for the beauty of today!

Playing music that matches how you feel is one of the easiest ways to change your mood. It's an easy way to lift your vibrations and feel good.

# Ah yes. Now I remember!

I said I was going to tell you about two dichotomies (that is such a lovely word). But I only told you about one because I'd forgotten the second. Well–now I've remembered!

You've heard or read about how we are all One–that we are all connected. Science has now proved that we are affected by the thoughts of others, even if they're thousands of miles away. We are definitely all One and every thought we think affects everything, everywhere.

Yet, 'they' tell us that we are unique and individual. In fact, I've mentioned several times, that you have a unique and individual resonance. So how can you be two different things at the same time?

But, it is so, because you are not one or the other–it's not a case of either/or–you're both at the same time.

At the spiritual, non-physical level we are all One, all part of the Divine: part of All-That-Is and yet, while we are in our physical world, we have a unique personality. We all have the loving qualities of our Soul in our essence, and our personality has the choice of how to express those qualities in an individual way. So we are indeed One with All-That-Is and we are also unique, individual and exceptional too.

And that's one of the other dichotomies of life. (I'm so glad I remembered before I got to the end of the book).

# And in conclusion

We came to earth to create happiness and joy and to experience our manifestations in our beautiful, physical world. It is such a magnificent playground.

Part of our awakening; our growing awareness, is that we are beginning to understand another of the great dichotomies of life–that we are All One and yet we are unique individuals at the same time.

Science has now proved that telepathy works and that anything that we generate is 'felt' by the rest of the world– literally every cell of every living creature reacts to our own happiness and joy and expands and evolves.

Conscious creation is not only the journey of our own evolution, but we're contributing to the evolution of our entire universe.

The more people who know about the Law of Attraction and how it works; the more people who decide and choose to create the things that make them happy, the quicker our world will become the world of our dreams.

The world is already changing fast. I do hope you are enjoying your journey, as you contribute to our amazing New World.

# A Parting Gift

To help you continue with your journey I have written a eBook called **'Seven Secrets of Manifestation** –a simple guide on how to consciously create the life you want.

To download this eBook for free, just go to www.rosetodd.com and follow the instructions.

I hope it inspires you to move 'confidently into the direction of your dreams'.